The History of Telecommunications

by Chris Oxlade

capstone

To contact Capstone Global Library please call 800-747-4992, or visit our website www.mycapstone.com

Edited by Helen Cox Cannons
Designed by Philippa Jenkins
Picture research by Svetlana Zhurkin
Production by Steve Walker
Originated by Capstone Global Library Ltd

Library of Congress Cataloging-in-Publication Data
Names: Oxlade, Chris.
Title: The history of telecommunications / by Chris Oxlade.
Description: Chicago, IL : Heinemann-Raintree, 2017. | Series: Heinemann
   first library. The history of technology | Includes bibliographical
   references and index. | Audience: Ages 7-11. | Audience: Grade 2 to Grade 5.
Identifiers: LCCN 2016058453| ISBN 9781484640357 (library binding) | ISBN
   9781484640395 (pbk.) | ISBN 9781484640432 (ebook (pdf))
Subjects: LCSH: Telecommunication–History–Juvenile literature.
Classification: LCC TK5102.4 .O925 2017 | DDC 621.38209–dc23
LC record available at https://lccn.loc.gov/2016058453

This book has been officially leveled by using the F&P Text Level Gradient™ Leveling System

Acknowledgments
We would like to thank the following for permission to reproduce photographs: Alamy: Purepix, 23; Getty Images: Dan Hallman, 20, Los Angeles Times/Al Seib, 26, Popperfoto/Rolls Press, 18, Spencer Grant, 22, SSPL, 16; iStockphoto: serts, 25; Library of Congress, 13; Mary Evans Picture Library: Illustrated London News Ltd., 7; Newscom: Ann Ronan Picture Library Heritage Images, 14, Everett Collection, 10, 12, World History Archive, 5, 6, ZUMA Press/Michael Quan, 24; Shutterstock: Alexey Boldin, cover (right), 28, asharkyu, 19, Everett Collection, cover (left), 8, 11, 15, 17, fztommy, 29, Matthew Corley, 27, Sidhe, 9, stockphoto-graf, 1, Viacheslav Yakobchuk, 4; SuperStock: Science and Society, 21.

We would like to thank Matthew Anniss for his help in the preparation of this book.

Table of Contents

Some words are shown in bold,
like this. You can find out what they
mean by looking in the glossary.

Telecommunications is the sending and receiving of words, sounds, pictures, video, and other information. We can do all this with the use of electricity, radio, and light. The telephone, **Internet**, television, and radio are all forms of telecommunications.

Today, you can see your friends on the other side of the world on screen.

Mail coaches carried letters between towns and cities.

Just 200 years ago, the only way to send a long distance message was either by sending it with a runner or by horse-drawn carriage. It could take days, weeks, or even months for a letter to arrive.

The first telecommunications machine was the electric **telegraph**. Telegraph machines were connected together by wires. Flicking switches on one machine made needles on the other machine twitch. The pattern made by the twitching needles spelled out a message.

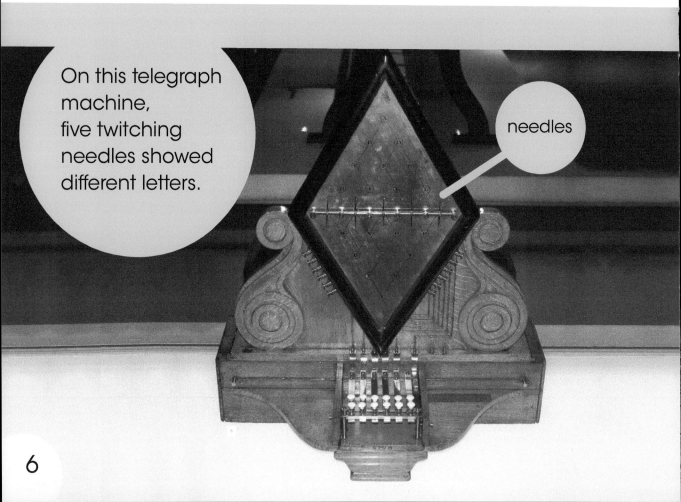

On this telegraph machine, five twitching needles showed different letters.

needles

Telegraph wires were held up on telegraph poles along the railroad track.

The telegraph was first used during the 19th century. Telegraph **operators** at railroad stations would send messages to each other. They used it to find out where trains on the railroad track were. Members of the public could send telegraph messages too.

In 1835, Samuel Morse joined two **telegraph** machines with just two wires. Alfred Vail was Morse's business partner. Vail suggested using a code of long and short **pulses** of electricity. The different pulses would be the letters of the alphabet. This became known as Morse code.

A telegraph operator sent long and short pulses of electricity by pressing a key.

International Morse Code

In Morse code, each letter is made up of dots and dashes.

When pulses of electricity arrived at another telegraph machine, the machine made short and long buzzes. The **operator decoded** the buzzes to make letters and words. Morse code was soon being used all over the world.

Scottish scientist Alexander Graham Bell spent most of his life working in the U.S. In 1876, he discovered a way of sending his voice along a **telegraph** line. He had invented the telephone.

Bell's first words on his telephone were to his assistant. He said, "Mr. Watson—come here—I want to see you."

earpiece

mouthpiece

The first telephones had an earpiece to hold to the ear.

Early telephone sets had a mouthpiece to speak into. This turned sound into electricity. The electricity traveled along a wire to another telephone. The person receiving the phone call had an earpiece that turned the electricity back into sounds.

Telephone **receivers** were not much good unless telephone lines connected them to other receivers. As more people bought telephones, more lines were hung above city streets. The lines went into homes and offices.

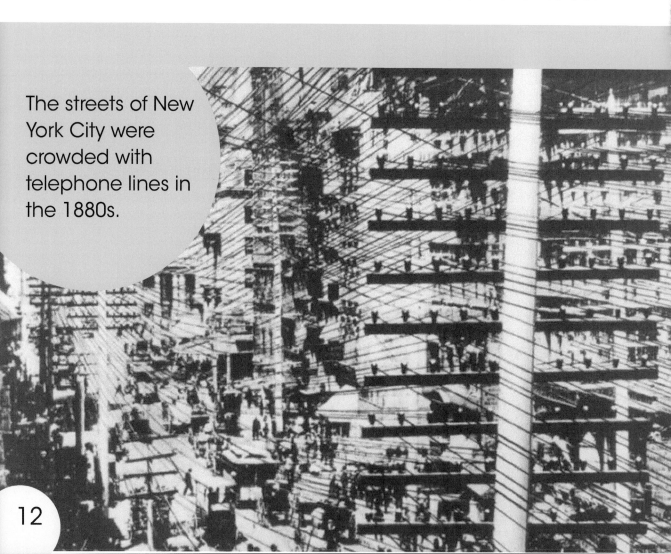

The streets of New York City were crowded with telephone lines in the 1880s.

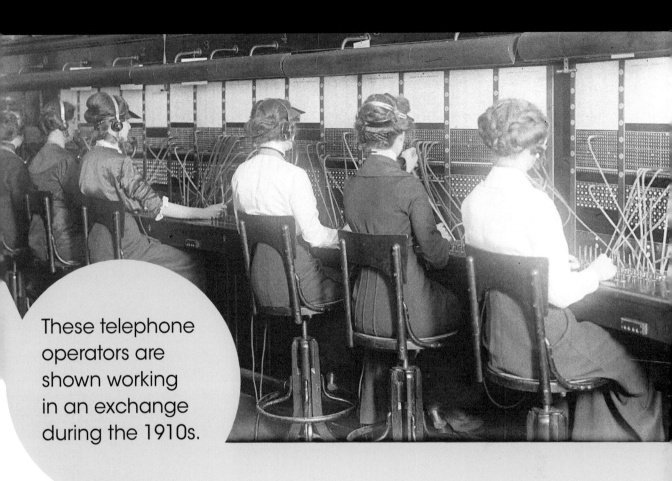

These telephone operators are shown working in an exchange during the 1910s.

All telephone lines led back to a building called a telephone exchange. An **operator** at the exchange connected lines together. This let one person talk to another. The world's first exchange opened in 1878 in New Haven, Connecticut. It had just 21 lines.

The word "wireless" was used when radio communications were invented. This was because radio did not need wires. In 1895, Italian inventor Guglielmo Marconi started experimenting with **radio waves** in communication.

This photograph shows Guglielmo Marconi with his early work.

Wireless signals were used to send out radio programs.

In 1899, Marconi sent a **signal** by radio across the English Channel. Two years later, he sent a simple Morse code message across the Atlantic Ocean. It went between the United Kingdom and Newfoundland, Canada. This proved that long-distance radio communications were possible.

15

Television is sending moving pictures from one place to another. A few inventors tried to create working TVs during the 1920s. In 1926, Scottish inventor John Logie Baird became the first person to make his television system work.

The first television pictures were not very clear!

The first television screens were very small.

Broadcasting is sending a **signal** to many different **receivers** at the same time. TV broadcasting began in the 1930s in the United Kingdom and the U.S. At first there was only one channel in the United Kingdom and a few in the U.S.

The first communications **satellites** were launched into space in the 1950s. Satellites send radio **signals** between places that are thousands of miles apart. This is how we get many TV signals, phone calls, and emails around the world.

This is the Telstar 1 satellite. It went up into space in 1962.

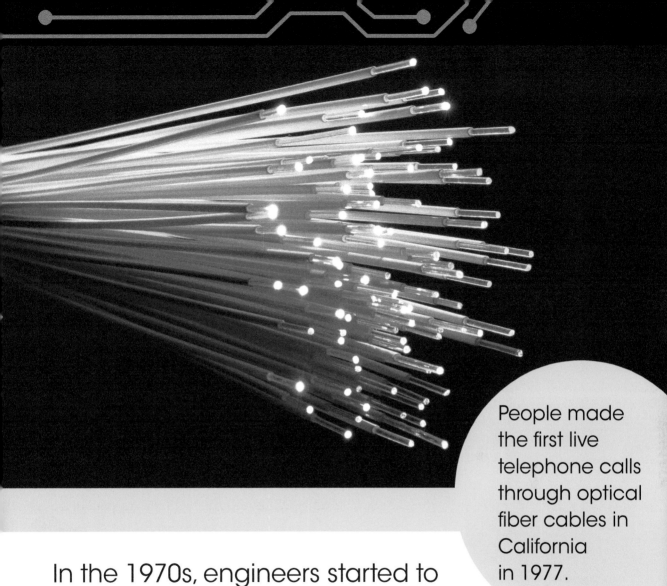

People made the first live telephone calls through optical fiber cables in California in 1977.

In the 1970s, engineers started to use optical fibers instead of wires. An optical fiber is like a very thin pipe with a glass core. Signals travel as fast as flashes of light through optical fiber **cables**.

Telecommunications companies made the first mobile telephones in the 1970s. Japan had the first working mobile telephones. The U.S. and some European countries quickly followed. Almost nobody used the telephones then—they were huge and very expensive.

The first mobile telephones were the size of bricks!

The Nokia 3310 was a popular phone in 2000.

Slowly, new **handsets** became smaller and their batteries lasted longer. Mobile **networks** spread wider so that the telephones worked in more places. The first-ever text message was sent in 1992. Text messaging did not become popular until the late 1990s.

The **Internet** is a huge **network** that links together millions of computers, tablets, and smartphones. It was invented in the 1970s. Scientists across Europe and the U.S. linked their computers together.

The first email was sent in 1971.

Over 3 billion people have access to the Internet worldwide.

Even at the end of the 1980s, only a few thousand people were connected to the Internet. By the late 1990s, when personal computers had become popular, about half a million people were connected. By 2015, almost half of the world's population was connected.

In 1989, British scientist Tim Berners-Lee invented a type of computer code called HTML. This allowed **Internet** users to read connected pages on the Internet. He called his system the World Wide Web.

Tim Berners-Lee came up with the idea of web pages.

Web browsers let us look up information on the Internet.

The first websites contained simple web pages made up of just words. Then photos, sounds, and videos were slowly added to web pages. By the late 1990s, all personal computers had a **web browser** so that people could search for websites.

Through the 1990s, mobile telephone makers gave their **handsets** more and more features. Telephones got cameras, games, and **applications** (apps) for sending emails and browsing the **Internet**. The word "smartphone" was first used in 1995.

The BlackBerry was the first popular smartphone.

Smartphones have apps that can do all sorts of fun things!

Modern smartphones are computers that fit in the palm of a hand. Applications (apps) let smartphones do different jobs. One moment a smartphone can be a clock or a diary. Then it can be a TV or a game machine.

Telecommunications of the Future

Telecommunications have changed a lot over the past 100 years. What changes will we see next? For a start, we will be using wearable technology more. That means we will have our **devices** on our wrists or in our clothes.

Smart watches may be used more than mobile phones in the future.

Smart buildings, smart roads, and smart cars could all be connected to the Internet.

All sorts of machines will become connected to the **Internet**, not just computers and smartphones. People can already access the Internet on household **devices** such as TVs. But in the future, almost all machines will be able to do this.

application (app)—a computer program that lets a computer, tablet, or smartphone do a job

cable—a wire for carrying electricity

decode—to change a code into language we can understand

device—electronic equipment made for doing a certain job

handset—a machine, or part of a machine, that you hold in your hand

Internet—a computer network that connects millions of computers to each other

network—a system that connects devices to each other

operator—a person who uses machinery

pulse—a short burst of sound, light, or wave

radio waves—invisible waves that carry sounds and images through the air

receiver—a piece of equipment that picks up broadcast signals and changes them into images or sound, such as TV or radio

satellite—an object used for communicating or collecting information that moves around Earth in space

signal—information sent or received by radio waves

telegraph—a system for sending messages along electrical wires

web browser—a computer program that lets you look at web pages on the Internet

Read More

Einhorn, Kama. *The 4-1-1 on Phones!* History of Fun Stuff. New York: Simon Spotlight, 2015.

James, Emily. *Alexander Graham Bell.* Great Scientists and Inventors. North Mankato, Minn.: Capstone Press, 2017.

Kalman, Bobbie. *Communication Then and Now.* From Olden Days to Modern Ways in Your Community. New York: Crabtree Publishing Company, 2014.

Internet Sites

FactHound offers a safe, fun way to find Internet sites related to this book. All of the sites on FactHound have been researched by our staff.

Here's all you do:

Visit *www.facthound.com*

Type in this code: 9781484640357